Older Woman Younger Man:

Timeless Attraction

Ingrid-Astrid von Anhalt

Table of Contents

Dedication

To all the couples where the woman is older than the man, this is for you. 🖤

In a world that clings to tradition and too often questions what it does not understand, you stand as living proof that love cannot be bound by numbers. You defy convention with courage and tenderness, guided not by expectation but by the spark you share, by trust, by laughter, and by the dreams you dare to build together.

Your love is not measured in years but in moments, in the strength of your bond, the joy you create, and the steadfast support you give each other again and again. In the face of judgment or outdated perceptions, may you remain unshaken, knowing that true connection transcends age and rewrites the rules.

Let your union be a beacon, a reminder that love thrives not because it conforms but because it chooses boldly, beautifully, and without apology. You are the embodiment of love's freedom and an inspiration to us all.

Acknowledgement

I am deeply grateful to those individuals whose unwavering support, encouragement and inspiration have been instrumental in the creation of this book. Thank you to my friends for their encouragement.

I thank all those couples whose honesty has touched my heart and motivated me to write. I appreciate you taking the time to share your thoughts and experience. I am grateful for your openness and your insights are valuable.

About The Author

Ingrid Astrid is an Australian author whose work delves into various layers of culture and the ever-evolving landscape of relationships. With a passion for writing, she creates uplifting and often provocative content that challenges social norms and invites readers to think differently about love, identity, age, power and belonging.

She is particularly interested in disrupting conventional thinking and inspiring meaningful reflection, encouraging her readers to question the status quo and embrace a different perspective on life. After a successful career in the commercial sector, she has exchanged the boardroom for a more expressive life, where her commitment to new approaches continues to thrive.

Timeless Flame

She moves with grace, a steady tide,

Years have shaped her, deep and wise.

He walks with fire, bold and free,

Drawn to her like waves to the sea.

She knows the weight of love's embrace,

He craves the spark, the thrill, the chase.

Yet in their touch, time fades away,

Heart to heart, they find their way.

No numbers bind, no rules confine,

Just whispered dreams and hands entwined.

For love is not a clock to heed,

But fire that burns where souls have need.

Introduction

Love knows no boundaries, especially when it comes to age. In a world that often raises eyebrows at relationships between older women and younger men, it is time to challenge outdated stereotypes and embrace the depth, passion, and connection these partnerships can offer.

Historically, society has been far more accepting of older men dating younger women, but when the roles are reversed, misconceptions arise. People question motives, judge intentions, and assume fleeting infatuation rather than genuine love. However, the reality is much different. These relationships can be deeply fulfilling, built on mutual respect, emotional maturity, and a shared sense of adventure.

This book explores the dynamics of such relationships: why they form, the unique joys they bring, and the challenges they face. Through personal stories, expert insights, and real-world perspectives, we will break down the myths and uncover the truths behind age-gap romance. Whether you are in one of these relationships, considering one, or simply curious, this book will provide a fresh, open-minded perspective on love beyond age.

So, let us set aside the judgement and explore the beauty of connections that defy expectations. After all, love is not about numbers; it is about hearts that beat in sync.

Breaking the Stereotypes - Love Beyond Numbers:
Challenging societal norms and myths about age-gap relationships.

Age-gap relationships are becoming increasingly common, yet they still face stigma. By embracing your love openly and proudly, you contribute to breaking outdated norms. The more people see happy, thriving couples who defy societal expectations, the more they will start questioning their own biases.

Love is often said to transcend barriers such as race, class, and culture, but one boundary that still invites scrutiny is age. Age-gap relationships, particularly those where one partner is significantly older than the other, often face scepticism and judgement. Society tends to impose unspoken rules about what is "acceptable" in relationships, and when a couple defies these norms, myths and misconceptions quickly follow. But why is this the case? And is there really an ideal age difference when it comes to love?

A common belief is that age-gap relationships are inherently imbalanced. The older partner is often assumed to be controlling or manipulative, while the younger is thought to be naïve or seeking financial security. In reality, many couples with significant age differences build their relationships on mutual respect, emotional connection, and shared values, just like any other couple.

Scientific studies suggest that while societal pressures may affect age-gap relationships, they are no more or less likely to succeed than relationships between partners of similar ages. Emotional intelligence, communication, and compatibility matter far more than the number of years between two people.

Age-gap relationships disrupt traditional narratives about love and partnership. We are conditioned to believe that couples should be in similar life stages, growing old together at the same pace. When one partner is much younger or older, it challenges this expectation. Additionally, gender dynamics play a role: older men dating younger women is often normalized, while older women with younger partners face harsher criticism.

Love is deeply personal, and every relationship is unique. The key to any successful partnership, regardless of age, is understanding, mutual growth, and respect. Couples who challenge societal norms often face external judgement, but those who prioritise their own happiness over outdated expectations find relationships that are fulfilling and meaningful.

In the end, love should not be confined by numbers. What truly matters is the depth of connection, shared dreams, and the ability to support each other through life's challenges. As society evolves, perhaps the focus will shift away from age and toward what truly sustains relationships: trust, kindness, and unconditional love.

The Cougar Myth – Deconstructing Stereotypes and reclaiming the narrative.

The myth of the "cougar" is rooted in outdated stereotypes that undermine women's autonomy and reinforce harmful double standards. By deconstructing these biases and embracing a more empowering narrative, we can shift the conversation towards one that respects personal choice and champions love in all its forms, without judgement or stigma.

For years, the term "cougar" has been used to describe older women who date younger men, often in a tone laced with mockery, exaggeration, or even disapproval. The stereotype paints these women as predatory, desperate, or merely seeking fleeting validation. However, such a narrow and often derogatory view fails to recognise the complexities of relationships, gender dynamics, and personal choice.

The "cougar" label emerged in popular culture, particularly through media and entertainment, where older women dating younger men were often portrayed as aggressive, domineering, or out of touch. Unlike men who date younger women, often celebrated or even admired, women in similar relationships are frequently scrutinised. These double standards underscore broader societal biases about ageing, femininity, and romantic agency.

Society has long accepted relationships where older men date younger women, often framing them as symbols of power, status, and vitality. Meanwhile, women who engage in the same dynamics are met with scepticism or outright criticism. This disparity reveals underlying assumptions about ageing, where men are seen as growing distinguished, while women are expected to retreat quietly from desirability and romance. The "cougar" stereotype is an extension of this outdated belief system, one that needs to be dismantled.

Contrary to the myth, many older women who date younger partners do so for the same reasons as anyone else: connection, compatibility, and genuine attraction. These relationships are not always about youthfulness or control but rather mutual respect and shared values. Additionally, many older women today are financially independent, emotionally secure, and confident in their choices, qualities that make them attractive partners, not desperate pursuers.

It is time to challenge and redefine the perception of older women in relationships. Instead of using derogatory labels, society should celebrate the autonomy of individuals to pursue love and companionship on their own terms. By moving beyond the "cougar" stereotype, we allow space for a more inclusive and nuanced conversation about relationships, ageing, and gender equality.

The Attraction and Connection

The attraction between younger men and older women is about more than just age; it is about compatibility, chemistry, and mutual respect. Confidence, experience, independence, and emotional maturity all contribute to why some younger men are drawn to older women. At the heart of it, relationships thrive when both partners bring something valuable to the table, regardless of age.

So, what draws older women to younger men? The answer is energy, passion, and a fresh perspective on life. Romantic relationships between older women and younger men have become increasingly common, challenging outdated social norms. While every relationship is unique, three key factors often play a significant role: energy, passion, and a fresh perspective on life.

One of the most appealing aspects of a younger partner is their enthusiasm for life. Younger men often bring a level of physical and emotional energy that can be invigorating. Whether it is a spontaneous weekend trip, a new fitness challenge, or simply keeping up with an active lifestyle, their zest for adventure can be contagious. For many older women, this renewed sense of excitement helps them break free from routine and rediscover their own youthful spirit.

Passion is a fundamental part of any romantic connection, and younger men often bring an intensity that can reignite desire. Unlike some older partners who may become complacent in long-term relationships, younger men tend to express affection more openly. They may be more adventurous, eager to please, and emotionally available, leading to deeper intimacy. This can be refreshing for older women who seek a love that feels dynamic and exciting rather than predictable and stagnant.

With age and experience comes wisdom, but sometimes life can start to feel repetitive. Younger men often bring a fresh perspective, introducing new ideas, interests, and ways of thinking. They may challenge older women to step outside their comfort zones, embrace new technology, or see the world differently. This intellectual and emotional exchange can be both stimulating and rewarding, fostering personal growth for both partners.

While the attraction may start with energy, passion, and perspective, successful relationships between older women and younger men thrive on deeper connections, mutual respect, shared values, and emotional support. These relationships often defy stereotypes, proving that love is not about age but about connection and compatibility. Ultimately, whether driven by adventure, romance, or personal growth, the bond between an older woman and a younger man can be just as meaningful and enduring as any other relationship.

The Chemistry Factor:

Understanding Emotional and Physical Compatibility in Older Women - Younger Men Relationships

When it comes to relationships between older women and younger men, chemistry is the driving force that determines whether the connection thrives or fades. This chemistry is not just about physical attraction; it is a delicate balance of emotional, intellectual, and physical compatibility that keeps both partners engaged and fulfilled.

Emotional compatibility, or the heart of the connection, is one of the most important aspects of chemistry in these relationships. While some might assume a significant age difference creates an emotional disconnect, the reality is often the opposite. Older women bring emotional intelligence, confidence, and life experience, which can be deeply appealing to younger men who are looking for a partner who is self-assured and emotionally mature. Younger men may also provide a refreshing energy, spontaneity, and enthusiasm that keep the relationship dynamic and exciting. This emotional exchange creates a unique balance, where the older woman offers wisdom and stability, while the younger man brings passion and an adventurous spirit.

While emotional compatibility is essential, physical attraction plays a significant role in the success of any romantic relationship.

Many younger men are drawn to older women's confidence and sensuality, as they often have a stronger sense of self and a more refined understanding of intimacy. For older women, being with a younger partner can reignite their own sense of desirability and adventure. The energy and stamina of a younger man can create a dynamic and fulfilling physical connection that enhances the overall bond between the two.

Beyond emotional and physical attraction, intellectual compatibility and lifestyle choices also play a role. A younger man who is ambitious and open-minded may be drawn to an older woman's knowledge and life experience, while she may find his fresh perspective and curiosity engaging. Shared interests and values also contribute to the success of these relationships. If both partners are open to learning from each other and growing together, the age gap becomes less significant. However, challenges can arise if life goals and expectations are not aligned; for example, if one partner wants children while the other does not, or if their long-term career and lifestyle choices differ significantly.

Despite societal stereotypes and external judgements, the chemistry between an older woman and a younger man often speaks louder than opinions. When emotional, physical, and intellectual compatibility align, these relationships can be deeply fulfilling and long-lasting.

Ultimately, the key to success is mutual respect, open communication, and embracing the unique connection that brought them together. Chemistry may start as an unexplainable spark, but when nurtured with understanding and compatibility, it has the power to turn into a lasting and meaningful bond.

The Challenges and How to Overcome Them

Navigating judgement in an older woman–younger man relationship can be challenging, but staying true to your love and values is what truly matters. With confidence, open communication, and a strong support system, you can overcome criticism and thrive in your relationship. Love knows no age, only the depth of connection between two people.

The most important thing is the bond you share with your partner. Every relationship faces transitions such as career changes, lifestyle shifts, or health adjustments. For couples in an age-gap relationship, being adaptable and supportive of each other's evolving needs is crucial. If your relationship is built on trust, love, and shared values, external opinions should not dictate its worth. Confidence in your relationship will naturally deflect negativity. If you and your partner are secure in your bond, others will eventually see the strength of your connection.

While love should be about mutual connection and compatibility, societal norms and personal biases can create obstacles. If you are in such a relationship, you may face judgement from family, friends, or even strangers. Here is how to navigate these challenges with confidence and grace.

If your family or friends are struggling to accept your relationship, consider having an open and honest conversation with them. Address their concerns, answer their questions, and reassure them that your happiness is not determined by age but by the quality of your partnership. Sometimes, people need time and exposure to see that their fears are unfounded.

Most negative reactions stem from deeply ingrained societal norms. Many people have been conditioned to believe that relationships should follow a traditional dynamic, where men are older or at least the same age as their partners. Others may assume that an older woman dating a younger man is a sign of immaturity, insecurity, or a fleeting desire for youth. Understanding that these views are based on stereotypes, not your reality, can help you take criticism less personally.

It is important to set boundaries with judgmental people. Not everyone will be supportive, and that is okay. Not every comment or judgement needs a response. Some people will never change their views, and that is not your responsibility. Learning to ignore negativity and focus on your happiness will give you peace of mind. If someone continuously criticises your relationship despite your attempts to address their concerns, set firm boundaries. Let them know that while you respect their opinion, their negativity will not influence your decisions. Surround yourself with people who uplift and support you.

There are many people in similar relationships who have faced and overcome judgement. Whether through online forums, social media groups, or local meet-ups, connecting with others who understand your situation can provide encouragement and practical advice. Having a strong support system can make all the difference.

Instead of dwelling on criticism, celebrate the strengths of your relationship. Age is just a number when it comes to shared values, emotional support, and deep connection. When you focus on the positives, others may begin to see your relationship in a new light.

Power Dynamics and Balance:

Older Woman-Younger Man Relationships

Romantic relationships between an older woman and a younger man can be deeply fulfilling and incredibly rewarding when built on mutual respect and balance. However, they also come with unique challenges. By maintaining clear boundaries, fostering independence, and valuing each other's contributions, couples can create a strong, loving partnership that thrives without falling into traditional caregiver–child roles.

One of the most important aspects to navigate is power dynamics, ensuring that the relationship remains balanced and does not slip into a mother–son dynamic. Age often brings more life experience, financial stability, and emotional maturity. While this can be attractive, it also has the potential to create an imbalance. The older partner might unconsciously take on a guiding or authoritative role, while the younger one might fall into a dependent position. This can lead to unhealthy dynamics if not recognised and addressed.

So, how is the 'mother–son' trap avoided? It is easy to slip into caregiving behaviours, especially if the younger partner is still finding his footing in life. To maintain balance, it is important to avoid making decisions for him or constantly offering unsolicited advice. Let him grow and learn through his own experiences. Do not take on a parental role in managing household chores, finances, or scheduling. Ensure tasks are divided equitably.

Set emotional boundaries. While it is natural to support your partner, avoid being the sole emotional caretaker. Both partners should be able to lean on each other. A relationship thrives when both partners challenge and inspire each other, emphasising mutual growth, respecting individual goals, and supporting each other's career ambitions, education, and personal growth. The younger partner may bring fresh perspectives, enthusiasm, and new experiences. The older partner may offer wisdom and stability. Appreciate what both bring to the table.

Further, maintaining equality in decision-making ensures that both voices carry equal weight in important matters. If one person consistently leads or dominates choices, resentment can build. Open communication about needs, preferences, and boundaries is crucial. Importantly, sexual and emotional intimacy should stem from connection, not control.

Avoid dynamics where one partner feels the need to prove their worth or maintain control over the other. Instead, focus on genuine attraction, compatibility, and shared values.

Why It Works:

Exploring the Emotional, Psychological, and Physical Dynamics That Make Relationships Thrive

What makes a relationship truly thrive? While love and attraction are often the foundations, the deeper success of a relationship depends on a mix of emotional, psychological, and physical factors that create lasting connection and fulfilment. Understanding these dynamics can help partners build a strong, resilient bond that stands the test of time.

At the core of every thriving relationship is emotional intimacy. This goes beyond romantic gestures and into the realm of deep trust, vulnerability, and shared experiences. Some key emotional factors include effective communication: open, honest conversations allow partners to express their needs, resolve conflicts, and grow together. Empathy and understanding are vital; the ability to see things from your partner's perspective fosters compassion and strengthens bonds. Equally important is emotional safety: a thriving relationship creates a space where both partners feel accepted and valued, without fear of judgement.

Psychological compatibility and mutual growth play a crucial role in fostering a strong relationship. When partners share core values, ambitions, and lifestyle choices, they establish a solid foundation for long-term success. A healthy relationship also nurtures personal growth and independence, allowing each individual to develop while offering support along the way. Additionally, the ability to regulate emotions and resolve conflicts with patience and respect prevents minor disagreements from escalating into larger issues.

While emotional and psychological aspects are crucial, physical connection is also essential in maintaining a thriving relationship. Affection and physical touch, such as holding hands, hugging or a reassuring touch, reinforce emotional security and intimacy. Sexual compatibility and intimacy play a significant role in maintaining closeness and strengthening the bond between partners. Additionally, spending quality time together through shared activities, travel, or simple day-to-day interactions keeps the relationship dynamic and fulfilling.

The most successful relationships do not rely on just one of these elements; they balance emotional, psychological, and physical aspects to create a fulfilling partnership. Couples who nurture these areas find themselves in relationships that are not only passionate but also deeply connected, supportive, and long-lasting.

By understanding and prioritising these dynamics, partners can build a thriving relationship that continues to grow stronger over time.

Sex and Intimacy – Keeping the passion alive while embracing evolving needs.

Age-gap relationships, particularly those where the woman is older than her male partner, bring a unique dynamic to intimacy and passion. While these relationships often defy traditional norms, they can thrive with a deep emotional connection, open communication, and a willingness to evolve together. Age should never be a barrier to a fulfilling, passionate relationship. With mutual understanding, communication, and a willingness to adapt, older women and younger men can create a deeply intimate and satisfying partnership. Passion does not have an expiration date; it simply evolves and embracing that evolution can lead to an even deeper connection.

As partners grow together, physical and emotional needs shift. In relationships where the woman is older, she may experience changes in libido, energy levels, and physical sensitivity due to hormonal shifts. Meanwhile, her younger partner may have different expectations of frequency, energy, or exploration. Addressing these changes openly ensures that both partners feel fulfilled and connected.

Honest discussions about desires, boundaries, and expectations are vital. An older woman may have a clear sense of what she enjoys in intimacy and sharing that with her younger partner can lead to greater satisfaction for both. Likewise, understanding his needs and desires fosters a stronger emotional and physical connection. Conversations about sexual health, preferences, and even non-physical forms of intimacy strengthen the relationship.

Passion is not just about the physical act of sex; it is about connection, excitement, and closeness. Couples can explore intimacy beyond the bedroom through shared experiences, adventure, laughter, and emotional vulnerability. Sensual touch, deep conversations, and acts of affection can keep the spark alive, even as physical needs evolve.

Sexual intimacy thrives when emotional intimacy is strong. The emotional depth that often comes with maturity can be appealing to younger partners. Older women may bring confidence, experience, and a deeper understanding of intimacy, which can make their relationships particularly rich. Younger partners, in turn, may bring energy, curiosity, and a fresh perspective, creating a dynamic that keeps passion alive.

Making It Last - Commitment and Long-Term Goals – Is it a fling or something more?

In relationships where an older woman is dating a younger man, defining commitment and long-term goals is crucial, as is aligning expectations. The dynamic can be exciting, fulfilling, and deeply meaningful, but like any relationship, it requires open communication and shared expectations to thrive.

One of the first things to address is whether both partners see the relationship as a casual romance or a long-term commitment. Sometimes, a younger man may initially be drawn to an older woman for her confidence, experience, and emotional maturity, while the older woman may enjoy the vitality and excitement he brings. However, if both partners are not on the same page about their future, misunderstandings and heartbreak can follow.

The signs that it is more than a fling include consistent effort from both partners to nurture the relationship, holding discussions about the future (including career, family, and lifestyle goals), and providing mutual emotional support with investment in each other's personal growth. Signs that it might be temporary include a focus solely on physical attraction or short-term fun, avoidance of serious discussions about the future, and a lack of integration into each other's lives (friends, family, and so on).

To build a healthy, lasting relationship, both partners should engage in open conversations about their goals and align expectations. This includes communicating honestly, with both expressing what they want from the relationship early on. Does the older woman want a long-term partner? Does the younger man see himself settling down, or is he still exploring? Clarity prevents future disappointments.

Differences in life stages can sometimes be a challenge. If one partner envisions marriage and children while the other prioritises travel or career growth, compromise or acceptance is necessary. An age-gap relationship may also face external judgements. Couples who stand strong together and reinforce their commitment will be better equipped to handle societal expectations.

Emotional connection, values, and shared visions for the future matter more than the age gap. If these align, the relationship has a solid foundation. As the relationship progresses, priorities may shift, so periodically reassessing goals ensures both partners remain satisfied and committed.

Ultimately, whether an older woman and a younger man are looking for a short-term romance or a lifelong partnership, the key to success is mutual understanding, respect, and aligned expectations. By openly discussing commitment and long-term goals, they can create a fulfilling relationship that suits both parties.

Financial Considerations – Who pays for what? Addressing money matters openly.

At the heart of any successful relationship, especially one with an age gap, is open and honest communication. Discussing financial matters candidly can prevent resentment, ensure both partners feel valued, and help build a solid foundation based on trust and mutual respect. Instead of letting societal expectations dictate who pays for what, couples should tailor financial arrangements to suit their unique situation and preferences.

Addressing financial expectations openly and early on can help avoid misunderstandings and foster a healthy, balanced relationship. Romantic relationships often come with various financial dynamics, and when there is a significant age gap, such as an older woman dating a younger man, money matters can become even more nuanced. In conventional relationships, it is often expected that the man will take on a financial leadership role. However, in an older woman–younger man dynamic, traditional roles may not always apply.

The financial situation of both individuals, their values, and their expectations all play a role in determining who pays for what. Therefore, it is imperative to understand each other's financial situation. Transparency is key. In many cases, the older woman may be more financially established, having had more years to build her career, accumulate assets, or establish financial independence. The younger man, on the other hand, may still be climbing the career ladder or managing student debt. Having an open conversation about financial stability, goals, and expectations can help both partners navigate expenses fairly.

One of the most common financial considerations is who pays for meals, vacations, and entertainment. Some common approaches are:

- The traditional split, where one partner (often the older woman if she has more financial stability) covers the majority of expenses, especially in the early stages of the relationship.

- A more equal contribution, where both partners split costs evenly, regardless of income disparity.

- A proportional contribution, where each partner contributes based on their income levels, ensuring fairness without placing undue strain on either party.

If the relationship progresses to cohabitation, financial arrangements regarding utilities and groceries should be discussed. Will expenses be divided evenly, or will the older partner contribute more? Does one partner own property that they expect the other to contribute towards? Are there expectations regarding savings and investments for long-term planning?

When one partner significantly out-earns the other, financial control can become an issue. It is essential to maintain mutual respect and ensure that money is not used as a means of control or obligation. Both partners should feel valued, regardless of their financial contribution.

Breakups and What They Teach Us – Learning from relationships that did not last.

Relationships between older women and younger men often bring a unique dynamic filled with passion, personal growth, and, at times, societal scrutiny. While many of these relationships thrive, others may naturally come to an end. No matter how painful, breakups can serve as profound learning experiences, offering invaluable lessons in love, self-discovery, and emotional resilience. Every relationship, regardless of its duration, shapes us in meaningful ways, teaching us about ourselves, love, and what we truly need to be happy. Though parting ways is difficult, the insights gained make the journey worthwhile.

For older women in these relationships, a strong sense of identity is often well established, but a breakup can still be deeply unsettling. It is crucial to remember that self-worth is not defined by a partner's age, attraction, or commitment. The end of a relationship can serve as a powerful reminder to embrace one's inherent value, independent of romantic validation.

Relationships with an age gap often bring together individuals with different life experiences and perspectives. When they conclude, both partners are left with a deeper understanding of themselves and their desires. Older women may find that dating a younger man encouraged them to embrace new perspectives, spontaneity, and even new interests. Likewise, younger men often gain wisdom and emotional depth from their older partners, fostering greater maturity in future relationships.

Age-gap relationships can also highlight differing emotional needs, and a breakup can provide clarity about what each individual truly seeks in a partnership. Was emotional availability a challenge? Did long-term goals begin to diverge? These reflections can lead to greater self-awareness and improved compatibility in future relationships.

One of the most powerful lessons from any breakup is learning to let go with dignity and grace. Holding onto resentment can hinder personal growth, whereas embracing gratitude for the positive moments shared can facilitate emotional closure and healing. Additionally, societal judgement can sometimes amplify the pain of a breakup, especially when others express scepticism about the relationship from the start. It is important to recognise that the value of a relationship is not determined by its longevity but by the experiences and growth it fosters.

Just because a relationship ends, it does not mean it was unsuccessful or unworthy. A breakup can sometimes bring out the judgement of others who doubted the relationship from the start. It is easy to feel like the end of the relationship is a validation of societal scepticism, but that is far from the truth. Every relationship serves a purpose, and just because it ended does not mean it was not meaningful or successful in its own right.

Love has no age, but timing matters. Love is not dictated by numbers, but the stage of life each person is in can play a crucial role. Sometimes, a breakup happens because of differing long-term goals rather than a lack of love. Understanding this can help both partners part ways with respect rather than resentment. Breakups, though painful, are steppingstones to a better understanding of love and relationships.

Older women who have experienced such relationships often emerge stronger, more self-assured, and more aware of what they want in the future. Younger men take away valuable lessons about love, emotional intelligence, and maturity.

Happily Ever After?

Defining Success on Your Own Terms in

Older Women Younger Men Relationships

Love does not follow a rulebook. Yet, when it comes to relationships between older women and younger men, society often tries to impose its own expectations. The age-gap dynamic, while still met with scepticism in some circles, is becoming increasingly accepted as more people embrace the idea that emotional connection, compatibility, and mutual respect are far more important than a number.

But what does success look like in these relationships? Does it mean marriage? Longevity? Or is it simply about experiencing joy and fulfilment in the moment? The truth is that success is deeply personal and should be defined on your own terms.

Not every relationship is meant to last forever, and that is okay. Some love stories are about growth, adventure, and companionship, even if they do not fit the traditional "happily ever after" narrative. Whether it is a passionate romance, a deep and lasting commitment, or a partnership that evolves over time, the success of a relationship is determined by the people in it, not by external expectations.

For some, success means marriage and family. For others, it is about maintaining independence while enjoying companionship.

Some couples may choose to keep things casual, while others commit to long-term partnerships without traditional labels.

Ultimately, love is about connection, not convention. Whether you and your partner choose a traditional path or carve out your own version of success, the most important thing is that you are happy, fulfilled, and supported. Forget the judgement, ignore the stereotypes, and focus on what makes your relationship meaningful. Your "happily ever after" is yours to define.

Live your own love story!

Real Stories and Lessons - Voices of Experience Testimonials From Couples Who Made It Work.

Tom and Barbara:
A Love That Defies Convention

Tom and Barbara's relationship might raise a few eyebrows, but for them, it simply works. Despite the 15-year age gap, they have built a strong, loving connection based on shared values, emotional depth, and mutual respect. They met nine years ago when Tom was 44 and Barbara was 59.

One of the biggest reasons their relationship thrives is their emotional compatibility. Barbara had substantial life experience and a deep sense of self-assurance that Tom admired. She was not playing games, was not insecure, and knew exactly what she wanted — qualities that Tom found incredibly attractive.

Tom, on the other hand, brought refreshing energy into Barbara's life. At 44, he had lived enough to appreciate maturity but still carried a youthful enthusiasm that kept their relationship vibrant. His ability to listen, adapt, and be open-minded allowed them to have meaningful conversations, laugh often, and support each other through life's ups and downs.

Money can often be a source of tension in relationships, but for Tom and Barbara, they approach it with openness and pragmatism. Barbara, having had a long career and possibly already retired, enjoys financial stability. Tom, still in his prime working years, continues to build his career and contribute his share.

Instead of following the stereotype that one partner is 'using' the other, they see themselves as a team. Barbara enjoys the sense of security that Tom's ongoing work provides, while Tom appreciates Barbara's wisdom in financial planning and investments. They complement each other rather than compete.

Of course, their relationship is not free from judgement, even after all these years together. Friends, family, and even strangers sometimes express their doubts or make snide remarks. Some assume Tom is only with Barbara for financial reasons, while others question Barbara's choice to be with a younger man.

But Tom and Barbara have a simple philosophy: they do not let outsiders dictate their happiness. They surround themselves with supportive friends and family who respect their love. When faced with criticism, Barbara responds with confidence; she has lived long enough to know that society's opinions are fleeting. Tom, secure in his love for her, does not feel the need to justify their relationship to anyone.

At the core, their relationship is about mutual respect, deep emotional connection, and shared values. Tom admires Barbara's wisdom, grace, and humour, while Barbara finds comfort and joy in

Tom's presence. Their relationship is not defined by their age gap but by their unwavering commitment to each other.

In a world obsessed with conventional norms, Tom and Barbara choose happiness over expectations, and that is what makes their love story so special.

Karina and Jordan:

Against the Odds

Six years ago, in a quiet little café tucked away on a side street in one of Australia's major cities, Karina and Jordan met by accident — or fate, as Jordan likes to say. Karina had just turned 33, a confident and self-sufficient woman who had long given up on the idea of love being a fairy tale. Jordan was 24, full of energy, ideas, and a kind of optimism that made Karina both smile and shake her head.

It started with spilled coffee. Jordan, rushing to grab a napkin, nearly knocked over Karina's laptop. Apologising profusely, he offered to buy her a replacement drink. Karina, amused by his flustered attempts at damage control, accepted. One coffee led to a conversation, which led to a walk, which led to an undeniable connection.

At first, Karina resisted. Nine years was a big gap. What would his family think? What would her friends say? But Jordan was persistent — not in a way that pressured her, but in a way that made her realise love did not always have to fit neatly into a mould.

Through the years, they faced the whispers, the assumptions, and awkward questions. "Is he mature enough for you?" "Don't you want someone more settled?" "What if he wants kids later, and you don't?" But every time doubt crept in, Jordan pulled her closer, reminding her that love was not about numbers.

They built a life filled with laughter, adventure, and late-night conversations. Karina, with her experience and wisdom, helped Jordan navigate his career and life choices. Jordan, with his boundless enthusiasm, reminded Karina that life was not just about planning but about living.

Now, six years later, they were still together, still holding hands in that same café where it all began. Karina had learned to stop worrying about what the world thought, and Jordan had proven time and again that love was not about age but about choosing each other — every single day. And so they did.

Claire and Anthony:
Timeless Romance

When Claire and Anthony met, she was 48, confident, and set in her ways. He was 35 and still full of energy and dreams. Their connection was instant; an unspoken understanding that transcended their years.

People whispered, and assumptions were made. "It won't last," some said. "She'll want different things," others claimed. But Claire and Anthony knew better.

They built their love on respect, mutual interests, and always compromise. When she worried about ageing faster, he reminded her that love was not measured in years. Claire says that Anthony always tells her she is beautiful. When he struggled to prove himself in his career, she was his anchor, believing in him when he doubted himself.

They have regular dinner dates but enjoy different sports. Anthony belongs to a basketball club, whilst Claire plays golf. They laugh at the little things; she likes jazz, he likes Country Western music. They learned from each other, grew together, and, most importantly, never let outside voices define their story.

A decade later, the whispers have faded, but their love has not. As Anthony put it, "Love is not about time; it is about choosing each other, again and again."

Anna and Julian:

Understanding and Shared Values

Anna, 48, never expected to fall in love again. After a difficult divorce in her late thirties, she had settled into a life she enjoyed — running her small business, travelling when she could, spending time with close friends, and being a grandmother to her daughter's young son. Then she met Julian.

Julian was 31, full of energy and optimism, with a quick wit and a passion for photography. He walked into her store one rainy afternoon, looking for a gift, and left with her number. Anna was hesitant at first. What could a younger man possibly see in her? But Julian was persistent in the most charming way, making her laugh, asking about her favourite books, and sharing stories of his travels. Slowly, her walls came down.

Their relationship was met with scepticism from others. Friends asked if she was worried about their different life stages. His family subtly questioned whether she would want children, knowing he might someday. But they did not let the doubts of others define their love.

What made their marriage work was not just passion, but understanding and shared values. Anna admired Julian's adventurous spirit, and he loved her wisdom and the calm confidence she carried. They found a balance between their differences: she introduced him to classic literature, while he pulled her into spontaneous road trips and photography hikes.

They talked openly about their fears and hopes. They acknowledged that they might face challenges as she aged before he did, but instead of letting that scare them, they made a pact to cherish every moment together.

They discovered that love was not about age, but about sharing, caring, and being happy every single day.

Famous Older Women - Younger Man:
Trailblazers

To the trailblazing women who defied convention and embraced love on their own terms — thank you. Your confidence, courage, and refusal to be defined by outdated norms have paved the way for others to follow their hearts freely. You have shown that love knows no age and, in doing so, I hope that you will inspire countless others to embrace happiness without hesitation. Your boldness is a gift to future generations. With gratitude and admiration, thank you.

Cher and Alexander "AE" Edwards — Cher's current partner, Alexander Edwards, is 40 years younger than she is.

Eva Longoria and Tony Parker — the actress and singer was married to Tony Parker, a French basketball player, seven years her junior.

Madonna and Ahlamalik Williams — pop icon Madonna has had several relationships with younger men. Most recently, she was romantically linked to Ahlamalik Williams, a backup dancer who is over 30 years younger than she is.

Demi Moore and Ashton Kutcher — the actress Demi Moore was married to actor Ashton Kutcher, who is 15 years her junior. Their relationship received significant media attention during their marriage.

Shakira and Gerard Piqué — the Colombian singer Shakira had a relationship with Gerard Piqué, a Spanish football player, who is ten years her junior, for over a decade.

Halle Berry and Gabriel Aubry — the actress Halle Berry had a well-known relationship with Gabriel Aubry, a model who is nine years her junior.